DESIGNER
SCRAPBOOKS

with

K&COMPANY
LLC

Left – circa 1923   Aunt Minnie & Uncle Fred.
Right – circa 1935   Grandma Carlman and
Uncle Fred.   The baby is Katie Arington,
Grandma's niece.

DESIGNER
SCRAPBOOKS

with

K&COMPANY
L L C

by
Kay Stanley

Sterling Publication Co., Inc. New York
A Sterling/Chapelle Book

CHAPELLE, LTD.:

Jo Packham

Sara Toliver

Cindy Stoeckl

EDITOR: Melissa Maynard

ART DIRECTOR: Karla Haberstich

GRAPHIC ILLUSTRATOR: Kim Taylor

COPY EDITORS: Anne Bruns, Marilyn Goff

STAFF: Kelly Ashkettle, Areta Bingham,
Donna Chambers, Emily Frandsen, Lana Hall,
Susan Jorgensen, Jennifer Luman, Barbara Milburn,
Lecia Monsen, Suzy Skadburg, Linda Venditti,
Desirée Wybrow

Library of Congress Cataloging-in-Publication Data
Stanley, Kay, 1964-
Designer scrapbooks with K & Company / Kay Stanley.
    p. cm.
"A Sterling/Chapelle Book."
Includes bibliographical references and index.
ISBN 1-4027-1057-7
1. Photograph albums. 2. Photographs--Conservation and restoration.
3. Scrapbooks. I. K & Company. II. Title.
TR465.S68 2004
745.593--dc22

                                    2004009147

Published by Sterling Publishing Co., Inc.
387 Park Avenue South, New York, NY 10016
©2004 by Kay Stanley
Distributed in Canada by Sterling Publishing
c/o Manda Group, 165 Dufferin Street
Toronto, Ontario, Canada M6K 3H6
Distributed in Great Britain by Chrysalis Books Group PLC,
The Chrysalis Building, Bramley Road, London W10 6SP, England
Distributed in Australia by Capricorn Link (Australia) Pty. Ltd.
P. O. Box 704, Windsor, NSW 2756, Australia
Printed and Bound in U.S.A.
All Rights Reserved
Sterling ISBN 1-4027-1057-7

Designer Scrapbooks with K&Company showcases intricately and artistically designed scrapbook pages and projects. The papers and embellishments used are from the K&Company series; however, any other brand will suffice to create these designs. On pages 122–141 you will find the Materials List, a reference guide to the papers and items used to design each project. To recreate an exact look, the K&Company product numbers have been included for your convenience.

Contents

THE Beginning

When a publisher approached me with the idea of writing a book, my first reaction was, "Are you serious? Me? Would anyone really want to read it?" Well, six months later, here I am sitting at my computer in the K&Company office 150' below ground (I'll explain our cave a little later), writing a book. And the best place to start writing is at the beginning.

(RIGHT) MY FAVORITE THINGS
designed by Kay Stanley

This photograph was taken when I was five years old. I designed the page around my "favorite things." I am truly a cat lover and currently have two cats, Buffy and Tyler.

MY ARTISTIC JOURNEY BEGINS.

I was born in 1964 in Kansas City, Kansas, to wonderful parents who encouraged my artistic talent from the beginning. The very first birthday gift I remember receiving was a ring-bound sketchbook. My mother gave it to me when I was only three or four years old; and while I know it didn't cost very much, to me it was invaluable. I quickly filled it with sketches, never knowing I was beginning an artistic journey that would, in many ways, shape my life.

My mother did more than simply encourage my efforts; she was an incredibly talented artist, and I believe she passed her creative genes on to me. In her spare time, my mother painted beautiful watercolor scenes and portraits. Her work decorated our homes, was welcomed as gifts, and sold at fairs. I often sat beside her, painting the exact same picture and learning the secret ways to make a tree just perfect, to wash on a sunset with multiple colors of paint, and make a building look like brick. It was truly fascinating.

In addition to sketching and painting, my mother introduced me to a variety of other creative outlets. She was a scrapbooker long before the art form became mainstream, and her scrapbooks were truly art.

MOTHER
designed by Kay Stanley

OUR FAMILY ACCORDION BOOK
designed by Kay Stanley

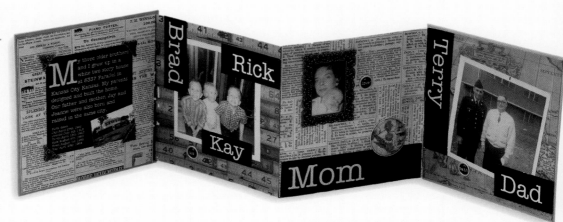

Creating this mini accordion book was a labor of love for me. I enjoyed searching through old photographs, remembering specific things that happened while these photographs were being taken. My older brothers and I were such hams when mom got out the camera. Choosing a variety of papers and stickers that coordinated with the photography selections afforded me additional time for reflection.

I have the scrapbooks she created as a young girl in the 1920s and '30s. We often spent time looking through them and working on new scrapbooks together. I received my first scrapbook when I was seven, and chronicled my entire grade-school experience throughout it.

We didn't have the beautiful papers and stickers that are available today, but there are photographs, journaling areas, and sketches throughout these early books. The albums have the heavily embossed covers you'd expect from years past. I think it's wonderful that this traditional look has proven to have such timeless appeal.

MOVING FROM STUDENT TO PROFESSIONAL.

When it was time for me to go to college, I took my scrapbooks and sketchbooks with me to the University of Kansas, where I decided to focus on the business side of advertising (although I did take a few electives in design). I was very fortunate that some of the design professors saw my artistic talent and took me under their wings, encouraging me to build a full portfolio and offering me a position on a university student design team called the "Arts."

After I graduated in 1986 with a B.S. in Journalism, this double experience of advertising and design helped land my first job as an art director for a Kansas City advertising agency. Over the next few years, the agencies I worked for provided experiences that helped me tremendously when it came time to start K&Company. I had the wonderful opportunity to art-direct catalogs for Hallmark Cards and Whitman's chocolates, and to create advertising and promotions for Campbell Soup, Procter & Gamble, Nestle Foods, and countless other companies over the years.

I found myself loving every moment of this fast-paced advertising world. It was here that I learned, from generous mentors, that there is more to design than just making it beautiful. Design has to work. It has to communicate and reach its intended audience. During this part of my career, I was also blessed to win more than 50 awards for my art direction and designs. Happy as can be, and thinking I would live out my professional days in advertising, I was unaware that one person would enter my life and completely change the direction of my journey.

I met Curt Seymour in 1990 and we began to date and work together successfully. Over the next six years, I helped Curt design gift products for his company, FSA Designs. The business sold products to the college and sorority gift markets. It was a side business for Curt, and a great freelance account for me. We worked on designing and manufacturing ceramic picture frames, photo albums, stickers, and more. Curt taught me how the wholesale gift business worked, and I helped him create products he could sell.

THE FIRST DAYS OF K&COMPANY.

In 1996, I designed a line of sorority stickers that Curt's business partners didn't want to invest in or add to the FSA product line. Not wanting to throw all that art time down the drain, I decided to take $10,000 from my own savings and manufacture this line myself. At that point, K&Company was born. Not long after, in June 1996, Curt and I came up with a novel way to personalize a frame using alphabet stickers. This concept, which we later received two patents on, was called "Frame a Name" and we sold it under the K&Company banner. Without much hesitation, Curt and I borrowed $100,000 from a local bank to finance the manufacture and design of the entire coordinating line of stickers and photo mats. We must have been pretty confident "Frame a Name" would sell.

We did very little research and conducted no focus groups, we just relied on our gut feeling that this would be successful. (This is not the business model a professional advertising executive would normally recommend.)

I remember how excited and nervous I was on the flight to Chicago for the very first K&Company trade show. We had just spent $100,000 on an idea, and I had no idea if it would fall flat or succeed. Fingers crossed, I took two days of vacation from my full-time job at the agency and headed out to setup our little booth in the Chicago Gift Mart. Curt arrived the following day to help with sales and to see if our investment would work. Within the first hour of the show, we took orders for "Frame a Name" from gift stores and Hallmark stores. What a relief! Apparently, we were onto something here.

FROM THE BASEMENT TO THE CAVE.

By August 1996, orders were starting to come in on a regular basis from the accounts we had landed in Chicago. Curt and I were both still working full time at our other jobs, and keeping up with K&Company was increasingly difficult. It was apparent that one of us had to go full time with K&Company if we wanted the business to grow. Since I also needed time to design more products, I was the natural choice.

At this point, K&Company was still a home-based business. We had inventory stacked on pallet shelving that Curt put in the basement of our house. Working around the clock to keep up, we would type the orders, pack the orders in the basement, and carry them up the steps one by one to the front door. We quickly realized we needed help and hired two people to work part-time.

CAVE ENTRANCES

(LEFT) *The entrance to Parkville Commerical Underground, home of K&Company.*
(BOTTOM) *We have three loading docks, two for large transport trucks and one for small delivery trucks.*

Over the next few years, our square footage rose from 2,500 to 6,500 to 13,000. In 2000, we moved into a 40,000-square-foot cave, 150' below ground in Parkville, Missouri. Since we moved here, we have expanded our building four times and currently have 150,000 square feet of space. The 25-foot-wide stone pillars that support the earth above our heads are quite interesting to see. (You're welcome to come visit us if you're ever in the area.)

By the time this book hits the press, we will most likely be underway building a new above-ground facility to help us become more efficient, and of course, give us more growing room!

One day, I remember the UPS truck arriving at our door. Boxes were filling up the entire front entry hall, dining room, and living room. There must have been 80 packages coming out of our house that day. One look around and Curt and I knew, it was time to move this business out of our house and into a warehouse.

In April 1997, we officially moved into a 2,500-square-foot office and warehouse space. We thought all that space would last us for a while. We were wrong. With the business really taking off, we discovered just three months later that the new facility was too small. With that, we began our constant moving into larger and larger warehouse spaces.

This board is centrally located in my office and is often my inspiration. I like to arrange materials, trims, ads, and photographs I have found on this board, where it can be studied over time.

EXPANDING THE K&COMPANY OFFERINGS.

Following the popularity of "Frame a Name," our introduction of the first 12 K&Company paper kits in 1999 and our bulk papers in 2000 helped us grow to where we are today. When we first began our scrapbook line, there was no such thing as a sophisticated, elegant, or designer approach in the craft and scrapbook market. That is exactly where I set my sights to give us a unique look—something that would truly set us apart.

I approached scrapbooking much like wallpaper and fabric companies design their lines for the home market. Coordinated collections of papers, stickers, borders, and eventually albums would come together to make it easy for the scrapbook consumer to create beautiful and elegant scrapbooks. Antique botanical engravings, classic vintage fabrics, and wallpapers immediately became part of the K&Company look. I'm delighted to say that many people have requested our designs for wallpaper, and that is a wonderful compliment I always like to hear.

Beautiful designs are part of the equation at K&Company. I have always tried to take our line to new levels, using techniques that haven't been used in scrapbooking before. For instance, we were the first company to sculpture-emboss scrapbook paper and matching vellum. The next year, we introduced embossed stickers and scrapbooks. Other scrapbook firsts for K&Company include embossed suede paper, glitter paper and vellum, leather embossed paper, specially coated fabric paper, and our patented "Frame a Name" personalized scrapbooks. I think it's safe to say that K&Company has become synonymous with texture and embossing in this field, and we're very proud of that.

Another thing that sets K&Company apart, I believe, is Curt's input. He has been instrumental in building the more masculine side of our company. You can see his touch in our popular military, police, firefighter, sheriff, EMS, and other special group gift and scrapbook products. Given his professional background, Curt also plays an invaluable role in conceptualizing and developing our collegiate products—everything from scrapbooks and photo albums to wooden gift boxes, picture frames, and paperweights.

FROM OUR HOME TO YOURS.

In keeping with the look of K&Company designs, Curt and I have a New England shingle style house, filled with period antique furniture, vintage fabrics, botanical imagery, and lots of wonderful flea-market finds. You're about to get an insider look; the scrapbook layouts and ideas in this book were all photographed in our home. The house is the backdrop for everything. Our stove mantlepiece, our hearth room, our library—it's all here.

Our typical weekend is spent visiting antique shops and finding unique things for the house and for the next K&Company scrapbook line.

When designing our home, Curt and I knew we wanted a traditional look. But we also wanted variety from room to room. Our entryway and dining room are very formal, the library is rich with cherry wood and casual formality, but our hearth room gives a very informal, almost folk-like feeling, with massive beams and a stone fireplace.

I design our scrapbook lines with the same basic approach. One look is not always enough. I try to incorporate very different designs—from our softer Antiquity and Isabella traditional themes, to our new Life's Journey eclectic look.

Surrounding myself with the best creative designers and illustrators is the key to our continued success at K&Company. Our in-house art team has now grown from just me to 14 wonderful hardworking artists, with varying experiences and backgrounds. Artists like Brenda Walton, Tim

KAY'S OFFICE

This is my office at K&Company. The back wall is actually one of many rock pillars supporting the ceiling.

Coffey, and our newest artist Elizabeth Brownd, add to our distinctive looks. I cannot tell you how much I have learned from each one of these incredibly talented people. I find it an honor that our company can work with each one of them: they are truly amazing.

It isn't just the creative talent that keeps our company growing at such a high rate. Everyone from the warehouse to customer service, from order processing to purchasing, from sales and marketing to our accounting department contribute to our success. We have a team spirit here where everyone works hard to achieve our goal of providing quality innovative products in the scrapbook and gift industry.

I'm also proud to note that the team effort is being recognized throughout the business industry. Recent honors for K&Company include the Ernst & Young Entrepreneur of the Year award,

and being named to the Inc. 500 list of fastest growing companies.

What's in store for K&Company? It's hard to predict the future, but you can certainly count on us to develop more exciting products you can use to create wonderful pages and albums. The list of ideas and products we would like to create gets longer every year. If only we had time to do them all!

There is one thing I can predict: Classic designs will never go out of style; they will look as beautiful in 50 years as they do today. My mother taught me that lesson, and I'm reminded of it every time I look at one of her beautiful scrapbooks. So let me promise you this: K&Company will continue bringing you classic designs, today and tomorrow.

I can also assure you of this: If I can write a book, despite those early misgivings, you can create beautiful scrapbooks! It's a journey you're sure to enjoy.

Family

"Who is that?" Thanks to my mother's steadfast dedication to journaling, our family never asks that question when we look through her scrapbooks and remember the good old days. My mother marked every photograph with a name, date, and description. There is nothing more important than the preservation of family memories. If there is only one thing you do consistently in your scrapbook, label your photographs and journal!

(RIGHT) FAMILY TREE
designed by Pamela Lange

The artwork for this family tree is an old lithograph that I found while antiquing. Family photographs can be printed in either black and white, sepia tone in various shades of brown, or color. These can be color-copied to similar shades and reduced in size to fit into the photo frames.

(LEFT) BIRTHDAY CARD
designed by Pamela Lange

ISABELLA ALTERED BOOK
designed by Jennifer Ditterich

Making personal gifts for family and friends can be made easy by using existing materials and adding personal touches to them. Embellishments can be added to the front cover of the album, changing it from a simple impersonable album to a family treasure.

Kevin, Colby & I had our family portrait taken last summer while visiting at mom and dad's in Syracuse, New York.

2002

OUR FAMILY

SUMMER IN SYRACUSE
designed by Jennifer Ditterich

The use of floral and striped patterns combined with straight and torn edges creates an interesting layout. The upper-right corner can be folded back to reveal floral paper.

(LEFT) FAMILY MONTAGE
designed by Pamela Lange

There are many varieties of frame styles and sizes from which to choose when doing craft projects. These frames can be embellished with paper and used for mini heritage photographs. Arranging them on matching paper inside a beautiful frame with ribbon trim can make a wonderful conversation piece.

(RIGHT) MY NIECE
designed by Kay Stanley

I enjoyed designing this layout of my niece Kelly. I used all embossed paper to give the layout a rich appearance. The double mat on the upper-left page was created using embossed pearl vellum.

Left - circa 1925   Aunt Minnie & Uncle Fred.
Right - circa 1933   Grandma Curfman and
Uncle Fred.   The baby is Katie Arington.
Grandma's niece.

(LEFT) GARDEN MEMORIES
designed by Pamela Lange

This layout was created using a rose trellis design on the left page. Similar trellises were very popular in the early 1900s. The use of rose paper and heritage photographs made this layout very nostalgic.

(TOP) ENGLISH ROSES CARD
designed by Pamela Lange

Adding dimension to the cover of the card with blocks of paper and stickers gives this card beauty. The frame may contain a picture as well as the greeting or poetry.

(TOP, RIGHT) ASHFORD LAMP SHADE
designed by Pamela Lange

Changing your lamp shades, seasonally or on a whim, is fast and easy. Choose a simple shade to start, then graduate to more difficult versions.

(BOTTOM, RIGHT) ASHFORD FLORAL CARD
designed by Sue Elred

This card can be used for any occasion. It is simple to make with an elegant look. Several of these, with matching envelopes, would make a wonderful gift.

23

Boy's Life

When we decided to do a theme for boys, I wanted it to be true to the K&Company style. "Tommy's Toys" needed a vintage look. I worked years ago with Stu Neyland, an artist for Hallmark Cards, and thought he would be perfect to paint the antique toys I had imagined. He was absolutely the right choice. Most of Tommy's Toys came from Stu's personal antique toy collection.

(RIGHT) CLASSIC
designed by Jenni Bowlin

All paper elements on this page were sanded with fine-grit sandpaper for a "worn" appearance. A brown fresco was used to stain the tags and other elements on the page. Little boys' favorite items were chosen to complete the collage.

(LEFT) ALL BOY MINI ALBUM
designed by Ruth Giauque

Antique toys were the inspiration for this mini "All Boy" album. Children love miniature cars, teddy bears, and pull toys.

(LEFT) RODEO DAYS
designed by Pamela Lange

Little boys dream of being cowboys. All cowboys need one thing—a bandana. You can achieve this tied-bandana look by adhering two pieces of paper together, then cutting a triangle with two tails in the center of the long edge. Tie the two tails into a single knot and your scarf is complete. Party invitations and cards can be made for young and old cowboys and cowgirls by simply mixing and matching patterned papers. Cowboys were thrifty and utilized everything available; adapt this idea and let your creativity go wild.

BANDANA FOLD-A-NOTE
designed by Cary Oliver

COWBOY MINI ALBUM AND TAG
designed by Cary Oliver

HOWDY PARTNER CARD AND ENVELOPE
designed by Cary Oliver

LASSO THE MOON
designed by Cary Oliver

ZAC

Zac's BEST BUDDIE[S]
known since pre-ki[...]
musketeers have so[...]
much fun!) during kin[...]

Zac's FAVORITE [...]
his own crafts. an[...]
time. Zac is so eag[...]
other day. which i[...]

Zac enjoys his BIG C[...]
also Zachary! They[...]
when his big buddy t[...]
slurpies.

GROWING
When I started kindergarten
I couldn't have felt smaller.
But I've been growing growing
And not just growing taller!

I've learned to read and learned
to write.
I've learned my numbers too.
And there are many other things
That I have learned to do.

Kindergarten's over now
But I am not afraid.
Because I know I'm ready
To enter the first grade!

for

(LEFT) ZAC
designed by Twyla Koop

*Graduation from kindergarten is a big day
and a great memory to document. The tags
list Zac's favorite things and the journaling
describes "growing."*

(LEFT) ZAC
designed by Twyla Koop

*Graduation from kindergarten is a big day
and a great memory to document. The tags
list Zac's favorite things and the journaling
describes "growing."*

(TOP, RIGHT) LOVE OF THE GAME
designed by Leslie Wilson

*What a perfect match—brown leather, a
baseball, and a mom who loves to
scrapbook. This mitt was made to appear as
real as possible by sewing the mitt together
with embroidery floss and leather strips.*

(BOTTOM, RIGHT) TODAY IS A GIFT
designed by Rebecca Robinson

*The joys of yesterday, today, and tomorrow
are reflected in Elijah's smile. Botanical
papers made the perfect setting with
gardens in the background of the picture.
Sanding was used to give the paper a
worn appearance.*

Girl's Life

Since I started scrapbooking as a young girl, it's fun for me to design layouts with today's girls in mind. Given our love for florals and pretty patterns, almost all of our papers are perfect for girls. In 2003, we introduced a new option: "Fabrications." This line consists of actual fabrics that are coated to give them more body and structure. The layout to the right is enhanced with beautiful floral fabrics.

(RIGHT) INQUIRE WITHIN
designed by Ruth Giauque

Little girls and their dreams inspired this layout. Her serious faraway look makes you want to "inquire within"—to know her thoughts and dreams.

(LEFT) BLUE JOURNAL
designed by Pamela Lange

Inquire Within

(RIGHT) OLIVIA'S GARDEN
designed by Brenda Walton

A frame of large cabbage roses sets off the mood for those rose garden photographs. Rose stickers are used in conjunction with the journal tags, while butterflies seem to flutter at the bottom of the page.

PINK FLORAL CARD
designed by Pamela Lange

ADDRESS BOOK
designed by Ruth Giauque

Children are always wanting to telephone or write a friend or relative. Make them their own telephone book and embellish it with their favorite things.

Hana and Mikenna's Address and Phone Directory

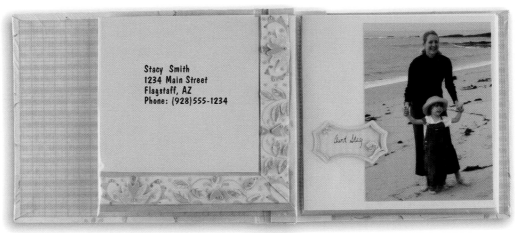

Stacy Smith
1234 Main Street
Flagstaff, AZ
Phone: (928)555-1234

(LEFT) COLLAGE FRAME
designed by Ruth Giauque

Simple embellishments on beautiful paper make a plain wooden frame a piece of art.

(TOP) CHERISHED FAMILY
designed by Debbie Turner

From their first meeting, these girls have been best friends. They love to dress alike, and a joint photography session was just their cup of tea.

GRANDMA'S ROSE GARDEN
designed by Patricia Gutierrez

Walking in grandma's rose garden is one of Laurel's favorite things to do. Using paper that reflects the image in the photograph creates an interesting layout.

To be yourself
in a world
that is constantly
trying to make you
something else
is the greatest
accomplishment.

-*Ralph Waldo Emerson*

TO BE YOURSELF
designed by Jennifer Ditterich

Meditation occurs in all ages, not just little girls. Being yourself is not always easy.

Brenda Walton

I have never met anyone more talented than Brenda Walton. Her artistic abilities continue to educate and amaze me. She can create anything—from beautiful, detailed oil and watercolor paintings, to breathless calligraphy and type design, to wonderful handmade cards. To top it all off, no one could ever be a nicer person or more supportive friend. I am honored to work with her.

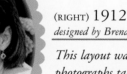

(RIGHT) 1912
designed by Brenda Walton

This layout was inspired by a series of photographs taken of Brenda's aunt as a young child playing in her nursery. Several complementary papers and patterns were combined to create a patchwork effect reminiscent of the time period portrayed in the photographs.

(LEFT) BELLA CARD HOLDER
designed by Pamela Lange

This little envelope can be used to hold business cards and makes a nice tote for small items.

(LEFT) BELLA MEMORIES
designed by Brenda Walton

This layout showcases a girl at age 15. The wreath pattern was found in a clip-art file and enlarged. It was embellished with sequins and seed pearls.

BELLA FAN
designed by Kelly Keller

Old fans that are found at garage sales, antique stores, and grandma's attic can be recycled into beautiful accessories. Use the fan as your pattern, and retain and use the handle.

DEAR FRIEND
designed by Brenda Walton

The inspiration for this layout cames from Brenda's grandmother's autograph album. It contains vintage photographs and mementos with handwritten messages from her classmates. This page was made to appear as if you discovered an open drawer filled with scattered memorabilia.

(RIGHT) JULIANA GIFT BOX
designed by Pamela Lange

Gift boxes can be easily made using old or new papier-mâché boxes. This box was covered with lavender damask paper and embellished with medallions and ribbons.

(BOTTOM) JULIANA STATIONERY
designed by Ruth Giauque

Stationery is easy to make using scrapbooking supplies. We used Juliana papers; the edges were sewn and then embellished with matching stickers.

(TOP) LOVE
designed by Kelly Keller

A variety of papers and textures were used to create a quilt-block effect, highlighting the seams with ribbons, beads, and dimensional flowers. The addition of glass beads to the flowers added a hint of elegance.

43

WORCESTER ACADEMY *Fall 1950*

THERE'S NO PLACE
MORE *delightful*
THAN HOME.
cicero

THERE'S NO PLACE LIKE HOME
designed by Brenda Walton

*The pictures were taken at the scenic
Worchester Academy in Massachusett in the
glowing autumn light. The rich colors and
historic patterns of these papers further
contributes to the warmth and love expressed
in these timeless portraits.*

A LEGACY OF
LOVE

Doug and Bumpa

Seashore Memories
Journal

Kaela August 2003

Former Berkeleyan Claims
Bride in New Zealand Rites

(LEFT) SEASHORE MEMORIES JOURNAL
designed by Kelly Keller

Cool colors were used for this seashore album showcasing a picture taken in late August. Sand from the trip was collected and put into a memory bottle, which is attached as an embellishment.

(TOP) NEW ZEALAND WEDDING
designed by Brenda Walton

Brenda's parents met and married in New Zealand, where her mother had grown up and her father was stationed during World War II. This layout commemorates their marriage and her mother's departure from her homeland. It was presented to them in a shadow-box frame for their 60th wedding anniversary. In order to preserve the integrity of the original documents, the newspaper headline and telegram were scanned and reproduced.

SOMERSET SHADOW BOX
designed by Brenda Walton

Tim Coffey

eartwarming and uplifting! Every time I use Tim's designs, I smile. Tim and I met at the New York Stationery show when I stopped by his booth in complete amazement. I had never seen such incredible textures used in painting, and knew Tim had to join the K&Company team. His honesty, commitment, and support of K&Company have never wavered; he is truly one of a kind.

(RIGHT) DREAMING OF DAFFODILS
designed by Kay Stanley

The rich yellows and golds in this paper made me think of a sunny day in a field of daffodils. Dimension plays a big part in this layout; there are three layers of papers used.

(LEFT) BEST WISHES CARD
designed by Pamela Lange

KELLY JENKINS
age 5

The BLUSH of your cheek

Your petal-soft skin

Your TRUSTING gaze

Your deep blue eyes

Your fat little tummy

Your MINIATURE toes

Just six of the reasons

That we LOVE you so

From: Girl

From: Girl

Our Newest

Blossom

Heather and Jacob
Easter Sunday

(LEFT) BLOSSOM
designed by Jennifer Ditterich

Children are wonderful subjects for our layouts, especially when you can catch that "special" pose.

(RIGHT) BLUE POPPY CARD
designed by Pamela Lange

(LEFT) DAISY BIRTHDAY CAKE
designed by Pamela Lange

What a fun way to have a birthday cake and treats for attendees to take home. Use die-cut cake wedges for the cake layers. Extra cake wedges can be used as favors for large parties.

(LEFT, BOTTOM) DAISY CROWN
designed by Pamela Lange

Every little girl loves to be a princess. This crown is made using belt tape which is covered with green floral tape. Green gingham ribbon is wrapped over the floral tape. The daisies, white toile, string of pearls, and lace trim are added as embellishments.

DAISY PINWHEEL
designed by Kelly Keller

Cutting two pinwheels and layering them together make for a full wheel. For added strength, make each wheel double sided.

DAISY INVITATION AND ENVELOPE
designed by Pamela Lange

This card can be adapted for party invitations, birthday cards, thank-you cards—the list is endless. Use a die-cut alphabet to spell out your greeting; then cut, glitter, and pop-dot the letters onto the card front.

53

Live

Laugh

Love

Kaela Amy Joelle
&
Rylee Dawn

HUNTER

(LEFT) DAISY DELIGHT
designed by Kelly Keller

A mixture of embossed and vellum daisy paper is used in this layout. The top frame has mitered corners with eyelets that have ribbon woven through them.

(TOP) HAPPY BIRTHDAY CARD
designed by Pamela Lange

This card features a pleated trim that can be achieved by first tearing the gingham paper and then folding knife pleats. The trim can then be placed around the outside of the frame, mitering the pleats around the corners.

(RIGHT) DAISY CANDLELIGHT
designed by Pamela Lange

This is a great way to jazz up an old lamp shade or add a personal touch to a new lamp.

Elizabeth Brownd

"Pure elegance" is how I describe the incredible vintage collages of Elizabeth Brownd. Elizabeth composes her paintings using a full collage of various papers, and then adds oil, acrylic, or watercolor depending on her subject matter. The result is stunning. I feel so fortunate to work with Elizabeth. Her passionate style gives us scrapbookers an entirely new way to look at and create a page.

(RIGHT) AS TIME GOES BY
designed by Jennifer Ditterich

Period stencils paper was used as the background in this layout of three couples enjoying a weekend outing. Matching collage paper and metal frame helped to create focal unity.

(LEFT) ALL OCCASION CARD
designed by Pamela Lange

(LEFT) FRIENDS
designed by Jennifer Ditterich

This beautiful page highlights a group of
friends. Time spent with each is cherished
and this page is a tribute to these
relationships. A mixture of embossed paper
together with elegant ribbon and charms
completes this page.

(TOP, RIGHT) LE FLEUR PURSE
designed by Pamela Lange

Creating a functional purse from a cigar
box, turned into a pleasant afternoon. There
is no wrong way to embellish the purse; if
you like it, it's just the right trim to use.

MINI PHONE BOOK AND TAG
designed by Pamela Lange

It is amazing what can be made from
scraps of paper and trim. The little phone
book and tag can be made in 30 minutes
and make a nice gift.

'TIS THE SEASON CHRISTMAS CARDS

Red poinsettia designed by Jennifer Ditterich
White poinsettia designed by Pamela Lange

The holidays are always here before we know it. Making cards can be a challenge; but with two papers, stickers, and ribbon or fiber, beautiful cards can be made in minutes.

NOEL
designed by Jennifer Ditterich

The wonder of Christmas and the beauty of the lights on this tree can be seen in the eyes of this little boy. This lovely portrait page uses a Christmas print and a coordinating striped paper.

Kaela
Eliz Braund

Kaela 2002

TRIPLE GIFT PACK
designed by Pamela Lange

Both this triple-gift pack and the striped frame (below) were made from existing materials. Boxes that you currently have on hand can be easily made into a classy gift by covering them with papers and embellishing them with stickers and ribbon.

(LEFT) KAELA
designed by Kelly Keller

Diamond quilt blocks arranged on the stencil paper with an assortment of tied buttons and ribbon were used to create this page. A matching pocket was made to hold mementos and journal tags.

(RIGHT) EMBELLISHED STRIPED FRAME
designed by Pamela Lange

Any frame can become an heirloom; choose patterned paper to match the theme of a room, cover the frame, and tie a coordinating ribbon at the top.

Heritage

any of our paper designs fit perfectly with vintage photographs that have been passed down over the generations. Our Isabella and Ashford paper collection was introduced in 2003 and uses many of my French toile fabrics and antique wallpapers. I love this paper so much! Beyond heritage, it's good for almost any occasion—from everyday life to weddings to pages for young girls. I use this line the most!

(RIGHT) PRINCESS ANA MARIA
designed by Patricia Gutierrez

Simplicity of design makes this heritage photograph a conversation piece. The simple use of dimensional floral stickers to create a frame around the picture made this layout an easy task of love.

(LEFT) ISABELLA CARDS
designed by Tamara Gilchrist

(TOP) ISABELLA ALTERED ALBUM
designed by Pamela Lange

*Albums can be easily altered to reflect your
own personal tastes.*

(BOTTOM) ISABELLA TREASURE BOX
designed by Pamela Lange

REMEMBER WHEN
designed by Jennifer Ditterich

*The message-board paper resembles a
vanity mirror, with pictures tucked
between the mirror and its frame.*

Grandpa and Grandma met before the war at a dance. When Grandpa joined the army, they kept in touch regularly and

in one of his letters he proposed. They were married while he was on leave and then he had to return to duty. Grandma

was able to join him for a while when he was stationed in Pennsylvania, but when Grandpa was sent overseas,

she returned home, waiting anxiously for word of his safety. He was a good writer, though, and always

kept her informed of his whereabouts. During this time, Grandma gave birth to their first child,

a son, and wrote to Grandpa with the good news. She also asked him to name the boy,

who had to wait patiently for his response. They both kept many souvenirs of this

time, but my favorite is a photo Grandpa sent to Grandma signed...

Love, Walfred

(TOP) HERITAGE ALTERED FRAME
designed by Pamela Lange

*A gathering of heritage frames makes
a beautiful addition to any mantel or
tabletop. This frame is embellished
with striped paper, metal photo corners,
and a bow.*

(RIGHT) HERITAGE HATBOXES
designed by Pamela Lange

*Each one of these hatboxes has one or more
patterns used for its base and a different
pattern used for its lid. Various trims in all
shapes, hues, and weights add variety.*

69

GRANDMA'S ATTIC

designed by Jennifer Ditterich

Tags were used to journal the passing of time in this layout. They may be placed in a pocket as shown, or attached to the page.

LETTER FROM THE PAST
designed by Kelley Brewington

Among the memorabilia that was found with these pictures were old letters and picture postcards, which were added to the page as well.

WEDDING TAG
designed by Pamela Lange

An unusual way to send out wedding portraits of the bride, or the bride and groom, is to incorporate them into tags. They are of a size that is easily used on a scrapbook page.

ASHFORD BOX
designed by Sue Elred

The Ashford Box was covered with paper and trimmed with border stickers. The journal tag centered on the front of the box was used as a photograph frame. The tag idea can also be used for a sentiment or a label.

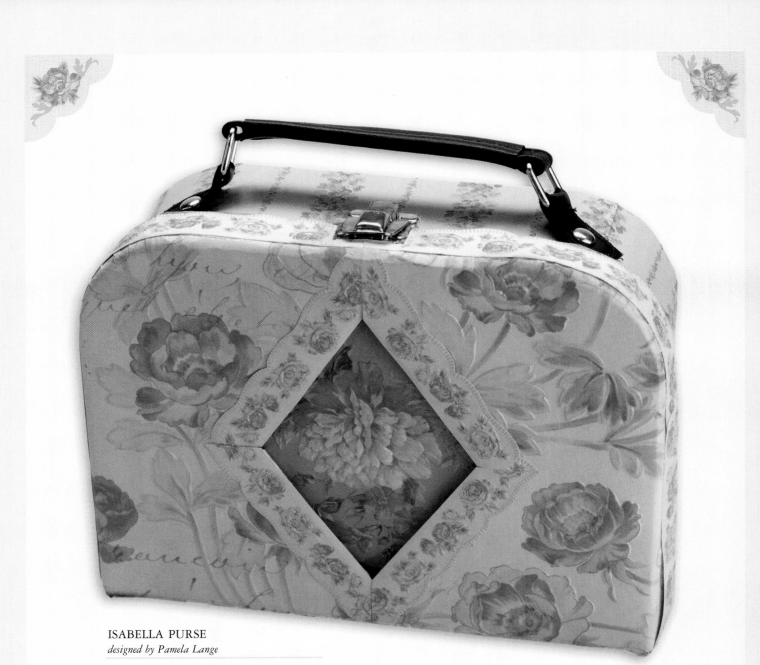

ISABELLA PURSE
designed by Pamela Lange

An old cardboard crayon case was used for this purse. The size and shape of this case are unique; the addition of a recessed frame in the cover made a great accent.

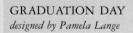

Mother

GRADUATION DAY
designed by Pamela Lange

In 1941, hand-painted photographs were very popular, as seen in this graduation photograph. A border punch was used for the frame, with a set-in panel of fabric.

WINDOW ON TIME
designed by Christine Kepler

At first glance, you see only a vellum-covered window. Upon a closer inspection, the windows open and pictures of a family appear.

(LEFT) ALTERED LEDGER
designed by Ruth Giauque

Ledgers are usually large and make a wonderful palette to embellish upon.

Wedding

Scrapbookers have told me that they use our albums
and papers more for wedding pages than any other theme.
Our embossed ivory papers,
pearl vellums, and traditional
florals are a perfect fit for
wedding memories. These
patterns are timeless and the
color palettes used allow you
to mix and match the styles
to create a layout that is
uniquely yours.

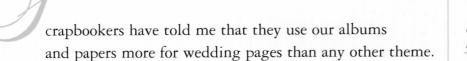

Mr. & Mrs. George Copeland
request the honor of your presence
at the marriage of their daughter
Margarite Annette
to
Thomas William Hollecker
on
Sunday, December 1, 195
at 2:00 p.m.
Chapel of the Cros
Kansas City, Miss

Marge & Thomas Hollecker
desire your presence at a
reception following the
ceremony.

Address: 2112 Maple Blvd.
Kansas City, Mo.

(RIGHT) WEDDING PORTRAIT
designed by Pamela Lange

*This picture was taken of my Aunt Marge's
wedding party. My mother is the last
bridesmaid on the left side. The colors and
patterns used for this layout were chosen to
depict the era of the photograph.*

(LEFT) WEDDING ANNOUNCEMENT
AND TAG
designed by Pamela Lange

Marge Hollecker

June 16, 2003

(LEFT) OUR WEDDING DAY
designed by Pamela Lange

The side-curtain effect for this layout was used to reflect the opening of a new window in the lives of the bride and groom. Rice thrown at the wedding was collected to keep in the vellum envelope.

(BOTTOM) FLOWERS FOR YOU
designed by Pamela Lange

This small box can contain nuts and mints for the wedding attendees. This box is die-cut and embellished.

Mr. and Mrs. Adolfo M. Gutierrez
request the honour of your presence
at the celebration of the Nuptial Mass
uniting their daughter
Patricia Ann
and
Mr. Raymond Fred Gutierrez
in the Sacrament of Holy Matrimony
on Saturday, January twenty-fourth
nineteen hundred and ninety-eight
at three o'clock in the afternoon
St. Joachim's Catholic Church
Fourth and I Streets
Madera, California

LACE-TRIMMED CARD AND TAG
designed by Patricia Gutierrez

(LEFT) WEDDING INVITATION
designed by Patricia Gutierrez

How often we wonder what to do with the beautiful wedding invitations that we receive. This wall hanging can be made in just a short amount of time, and makes a wonderful gift for the couple's new home.

(RIGHT) WEDDING DAY PICTURE
designed by Patricia Gutierrez

81

You're invited to a Wedding Shower

For: *Karah & Thomas*

When: *May 11*

Time: *2:00 p.m.*

Where: *9817 Colby*

RSVP *548-2116*

GIFT CARDS AND ENVELOPES
designed by Pamela Lange

Wedding Day

Mr. & Mrs. Thomas Wilson
request the honor of your presence
at the marriage of their daughter
Angela Marie
to
...nas William Pa...
...day, March...
2:00 p.m...
...el of t...
...City,...

(LEFT AND BOTTOM) TO LOVE, HONOR,
AND CHERISH
designed by Lori Bergman

*What a great post-wedding gift for the
bride, the couple's families, and other
wedding participants. This is a creative
way to use all of the candid photographs
taken at the wedding and reception.*

ALTERED WEDDING ALBUM
designed by Pamela Lange

The scrapbook world now is all about altering items. The right-hand portion of this album was covered with a favorite paper. A ribbon was added where the paper meets the fabric.

You were made perfectly to be loved — and surely I have loved you, in the idea of you, my whole life long.

Elizabeth Barrett Browning

Baby

My youngest nephew, Jack, follows a long line of nephews, including Bryan, Rodney, Jeff, Clay, Tyler, and Pete. You would think one girl would slide in there! Jack inspired the page shown to the right. Illustrator Jo Ackley painted those cozy little stuffed animals and I can't imagine anything cuter. It didn't take long to expand this line to include scrapbooks, photo albums, and frames.

(RIGHT) BABY JACK
designed by Kay Stanley

This simple layout is achieved by overlapping the paper animals on top of each other for dimension, then embellishing with ribbon and buttons.

(LEFT) HUMPTY DUMPTY CARD
designed by Pamela Lange

Mothers usually have a lot of memorabilia from the births of their children. This little accordion book pulls together a few of these precious items, and is the right size to be easily carried and shown.

(TOP) BABY LAMP
designed by Pamela Lange

This lamp reminds me of an old TV lamp with moving parts inside. This style of lamp can be found at discount stores. Remove the outside shade, replace it with paper, and your lamp is finished.

Lillian

Nicole

Jackson

(TOP) FIELD OF DREAMS
designed by Pamela Lange

The design of this paper, with its mural effect, made me think of sleepy afternoons and sweet babies. The lamb and meadow flowers have been embellished with fibers.

OUR SWEET GRAND BABIES...

bring joy everyday to Jay and myself.

Joshua, Megan and baby Molly spend

every afternoon with us since Patti went

back to work at Thompson & Black

law firm. It brings us pleasure to help out

Patti, but more pleasure to have the

quality time with our three little angels.

OUR SWEET GRANDBABIES
designed by Kay Stanley

The easy flow from page to page is achieved by applying a continuous border around the two pages. Spring flowers are spread randomly across the top of the layout. Above is the pattern for the floral design. Enlarge the pattern to the desired size.

NOTES OF LOVE

To Our Dear Baby Girl...

From Mot... ...rom Father

Rylee Dawn

2002

NOTES OF LOVE
designed by Kelly Keller

So many thoughts run through our minds
when a new baby is born. New fathers
and mothers each have their own special
hopes and dreams for their child. In this
layout, there are envelopes and note cards
provided for parental thoughts.

It's a Boy!

BABY BOY CARD
designed by Pamela Lange

Any letter can be made using this technique. Select a letter style, enlarge to the size of the card you wish to create, and cut a pattern. Make an additional pattern in a smaller size for the patterned overlay.

Men's Club

I would say our company was overdue when it came to offering scrapbook collections based on more masculine themes. We certainly made up for that. When we decided to do a men's theme, we jumped in with both feet. From sports themes to rich classic plaids and stripes, our line gives scrapbookers handsome options for creating the ultimate memory book for their husbands, sons, fathers, and friends.

(RIGHT) **MY BEST FRIEND**
designed by Debbie Turner

Fall is so beautiful with all of the changing colors. Brown leather and plaid fabric make a wonderful background for the mounted trophy.

(LEFT) **FOREST JOURNAL**
designed by Pamela Lange

Jason Bland

MY HERO
designed by Debbie Turner

This layout is made by layering patterned paper with chalk-trimmed cardstock and embellishing with hand-sewing and tags. Sepia-toned photographs are the perfect match for this color palette.

Hero

(TOP, LEFT) WILLIAM "PETE" ROGERS
designed by Pamela Lange

Elements from a camouflage uniform were
re-created from paper to form a frame and
a memorabilia pocket. These were sewn
and creased for a more natural appearance.

(BOTTOM, LEFT) OUR MARINES
designed by Pamela Lange

This layout can be designed for any branch
of the military by simply changing the title
and embellishments. The second page can
be a collage of memorabilia.

(ABOVE) TERRY STANLEY
designed by Pamela Lange

This layout is of my older brother Terry
Stanley. This collage is simple and easily
made. Choose a base page, layer a military
sheet along with decorative mesh, and add
a matted picture. Embellish with a label
holder, tag, and service awards.

Life's Journey

Creating this line was a truly delightful journey itself. It was incredibly rewarding to find antiques at home that could be used for art. Digging through old boxes was a treasure hunt that yielded beautiful documents, including land deeds passed down in my family for generations. What a thrill to see these heirlooms become paper and sticker designs! We also had fun scouring local antique stores and archives.

(LEFT AND RIGHT) MY SISTER, MY FRIEND
designed by Kay Stanley

I love the old photographs I found of my mother and her sister Rita. I used papers with a heritage look in combination with an antique clock overlay. The use of a clock gives the layout a feeling of passing time.

100

ELEMENTS OF YOU
designed by Tracey Niehues

A coin holder makes a wonderful display case for this spread. Insert pictures, poetry, journaling, stickers, and found items to create a truly interesting keepsake. The cover may also be embellished.

Simplicity is making the journey of this life with just baggage enough.

CHICAGO
DEC 6
5-PM
10
ILL.

MEMORIES

TRAVEL

TRAVEL SIMPLICITY
designed by Tracey Niehues

This gate-fold album has been embellished with file pockets on the front to hold maps, postcards, and other collectibles. The small journal at the top has been torn, aged, and sewn with a zigzag stitch. The use of many styles of text added variety and interest to the cover.

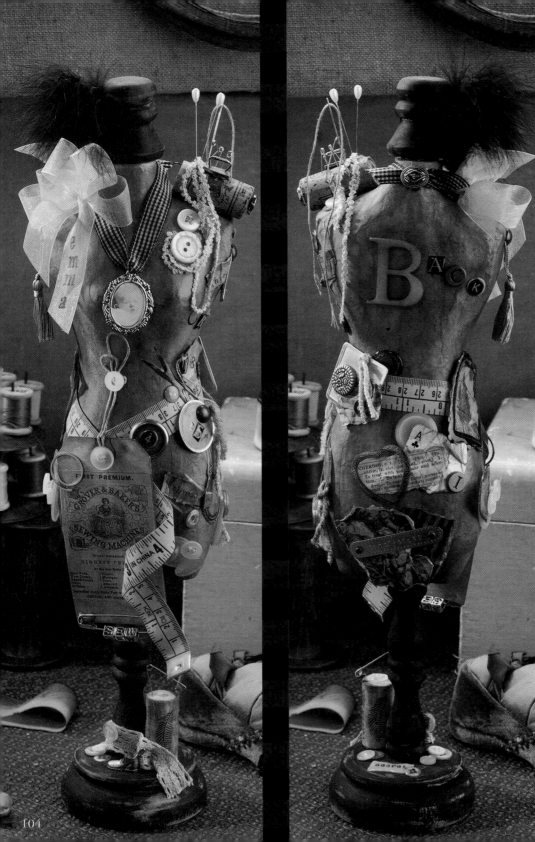

(LEFT) ALTERED SEWING FORM
designed by Holly Nelsen

The altering of a seamstress form is a unique way to show off small collectibles. Attach pieces of a favorite paper, ticket stubs, old keys, and buttons. The supply list is limitless. The papier-mâché form can be stained with walnut ink or a stamp pad if an aged appearance is preferred.

(RIGHT) BITS AND PIECES
designed by Tracey Niehues

Puzzle pieces, which have been stained, painted, and tied with ribbon, embellish the bottom of this page. Tissue has been crumpled, stained, and sewn for trim around the photograph. These techniques can be combined with embossed vellum and text to create interesting pages to surround a photograph.

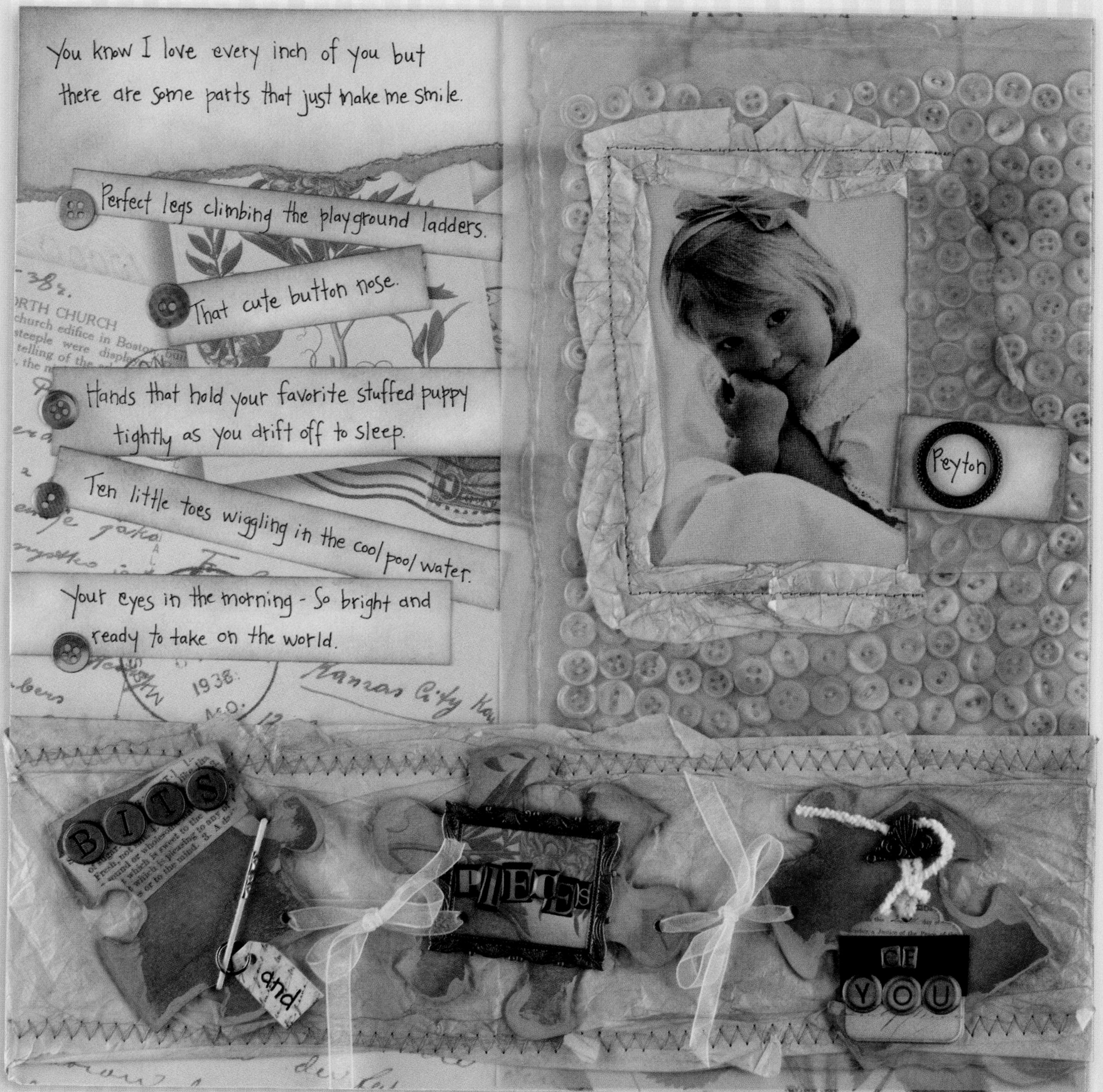

You know I love every inch of you but there are some parts that just make me smile.

Perfect legs climbing the playground ladders.

That cute button nose.

Hands that hold your favorite stuffed puppy tightly as you drift off to sleep.

Ten little toes wiggling in the cool pool water.

Your eyes in the morning - So bright and ready to take on the world.

Peyton

BITS and PIECES OF YOU

MY GRANDMOTHER
designed by Tracey Niehues

*Fabric was used for the base of these two
pages. The pages were stained and sewn to
give an aged appearance. Two pockets run
the entire width of the second page to hold
pictures and cards. Tags and other
memorablia were attached to the outside of
the pockets, using clothespins, bobby pins,
decorative paperclips, and buttons. Period
buttons and tassels were added to the
corner of the portrait.*

PHOTO FILE
designed by Tracey Niehues

An altered cancelled-check file becomes a fabulous Photo File by creating a fabric pocket and attaching it with brads to the front of the file. An ink-jet printer can be used when printing on some fabrics. Cover the inside cover and "junk it up" with papers and stickers.

This layout shows my son Kyle, myself, my mother, and my grandmother. I liked doing a layout where the ages of the participants in the photographs are close to the same age, yet span many years.

(TOP) WINDOW OF THE SOUL ACCORDION BOOK
designed by Tracey Niehues

The cover of this accordion book shows a child's framed face with random words which say "The eyes are the window of the soul." The frame is placed on a torn and crumpled piece of newspaper print.

PURSE
designed by Tracey Niehues

(RIGHT) DOMINO TAG BOOK
designed by Tracey Niehues

This little booklet comes with a button closure that can be furthur embellished with fibers and ribbons. This booklet is devoted to school days; reading, writing, and arithmetic.

GREAT, GREAT, GREAT-GRANDFATHER BURNSIDE
designed by Cary Oliver

To create a similar frame, tear pieces of newspaper print and layer onto a chipboard frame. When the frame is totally covered with paper, use contact paper to seal the pieces and provide a clear coating. A flipable photograph in the frame allows plenty of room for journaling and showcasing memorabilia underneath.

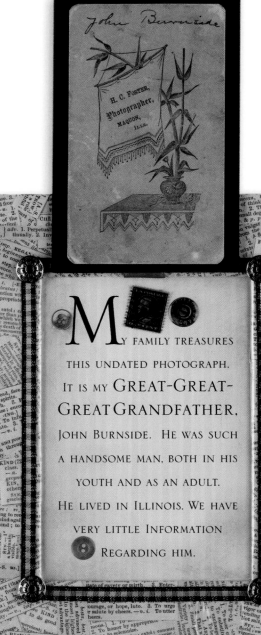

My Family Treasures this undated photograph. It is my GREAT-GREAT-GREAT Grandfather, John Burnside. He was such a handsome man, both in his youth and as an adult. He lived in Illinois. We have very little information regarding him.

This portrait was taken at the Covington Gallery in 1864. The man is my GREAT-GREAT-GREAT GRANDFATHER, John Burnside. The reverse side of the original portrait has a cancelled stamp dated August 11, 1864.

John Burnside

111

RULER JOURNAL
designed by Melanie Cantrell

THE TOUR
designed by Pamela Lange

QUILT MEMORIES
designed by Pamela Lange

ALTERED BOXES
designed by Pamela Lange

The boxes were covered with three different patterns; the inside of each lid sports a coordinating paper. The bottom edge of the tag was border punched.

113

SOMETHING OLD, SOMETHING NEW
*designed by Melanie Cantrell, Pamela Lange,
and Tracey Niehues*

*This coat rack is located in the mudroom of
our home. It is a great place to display
antiques, lost keys, and in this instance,
altered tags.*

Holiday

I always enjoy decorating our home for the holidays. It's a treat to bring out the various garlands, pinecones, and antique ornaments for the tree. This year I decided to dress up the mantel over our stove with alphabet tags spelling out "Merry Christmas." Pam Lange, who has worked with me since almost the beginning of K&Company, helped put the final touches on this special new Christmas decoration.

(RIGHT) CHRISTMAS GARLAND
designed by Kay Stanley

My favorite room in our home is our kitchen. I love the hearth over our range and decided that it would be one of the focal points of my Christmas decorating. These tags were made from a mix and match of color-coordinated papers and border stickers, embellished with buttons and lace. I printed each letter on my computer and tied them to the cord with gold string.

(LEFT) CHRISTMAS CARD
designed by Melanie Cantrell

ADVENT WREATH
designed by Lori Bergman

CHRISTMAS CARD AND ORNAMENT
designed by Sue Elred

Christmas just is not complete without a calendar, cards, and ornaments. What fun it is to have handmade decorations that can be handed down from generation to generation.

BUTTON PLACE SETTINGS
designed by Judi Vaughan

The heart (left) and sconce (right) were made to use on chair backs for afternoon tea or for a special occasion. Each one would have a small place card placed inside. After the festivities end, the guests would take these keepsakes home with them. The buttons around the heart were sewn with a crochet stitch.

Materials List

Page 8
MY FAVORITE THINGS
designed by Kay Stanley
Papers:
- 1 sheet ivory floral pattern (#635548)
- 1 sheet ivory quilt pattern (#634701)
- 1 sheet olive and peach stripe pattern (#635531)
- 1 sheet olive cardstock (#630963)
- 1 sheet olive floral pattern (#635555)
- 1 sheet olive floral stripe pattern (#635500)
- 1 sheet script pattern (#635975)
Materials:
- 12 assorted buttons
- Ivory fabric scrap

- Ivory trim
- Shear ivory ribbon

Page 10
MOTHER
designed by Kay Stanley
Papers:
- 1 sheet floral stripe pattern (#635500)
- 1 sheet olive floral pattern (#635555)
- 1 sheet script pattern (#635975)
- 1 sheet toile pattern (#635494)
Materials:
- 12"x12" cream frame (#390027)
- Cream button
- Mother sticker (#554405)
- Pink ribbon

Page 11
OUR FAMILY ACCORDION BOOK
designed by Kay Stanley

Papers:
- 1 sheet black letters pattern (#563537)
- 1 sheet dictionary pattern (#636279)
- 1 sheet furniture ad pattern (#636460)
- 1 sheet old world map pattern (#636354)
- 1 sheet postcard pattern (#636262)
- 1 sheet tape measure pattern (#636552)
Materials:
- Kraft accordion book (#536258)
- Metal photo corners (#558014)
- Rectangle frame (#563452)
- Round floral button (#558908)
- Round frame (#563414)
- Typewriter words (#558137)

Page 17
OUR FAMILY TREE
designed by Pamela Lange
Papers:
- 3 sheets family tree pattern (#638426)

Materials:
- 12"x12" black sculptured frame (#390256)
- Gold ribbon

Page 18
ISABELLA ALTERED BOOK
designed by Jennifer Ditterich
Materials:
- 6"x6" album (#534049)
- Cream ribbon
- Domed frame (#557000)
- Key charm (#558373)
- Metal frame (#558007)

Page 19
SUMMER IN SYRACUSE
designed by Jennifer Ditterich
Papers:
- 1 sheet floral pattern (#635548)
- 1 sheet green floral vellum (#634428)
- 1 sheet green linen pattern (#635524)
- 1 sheet ivory quilt pattern (#635043)

- 1 sheet olive and pink stripe pattern (#635531)

Materials:
- Floral journal tags (#552807)
- Floral stickers (#552845)
- Green border and corner stickers (#552821)
- Green ribbon

Page 20
FAMILY MONTAGE
designed by Pamela Lange
Papers:
- 1 sheet floral stripe pattern (#635500)
- 1 sheet olive floral pattern (#635555)

Materials:
- 4 assorted mini frames
- 12"x12" silver frame (#390270)
- Copper ribbon

Page 21
MY NIECE
designed by Kay Stanley
Papers:
- 1 sheet floral pearl vellum (#633902)
- 1 sheet floral vellum (#633391)
- 1 sheet ivory embossed pattern (#633889)
- 2 sheets beige pattern (#633407)

Materials:
- Die-cut frames (#651098)
- Floral journal tag stickers (#552661)
- Floral stickers (#552647)

- Floral vine border stickers (#552678)
- Ivory tassel
- Olive ribbon
- Rose ribbon

Page 22
GARDEN MEMORIES
designed by Pamela Lange
Papers:
- 1 sheet green pattern (#632752)
- 1 sheet tan pattern (#633926)
- 2 sheets border pattern (#633919)
- 2 sheets floral pattern (#633384)

Materials:
- 2 die-cut frames (#651098)
- Cream ribbon

Page 23
ENGLISH ROSES CARD
designed by Pamela Lange
Papers:
- 1 sheet beige pattern (#633872)
- 1 sheet clear vellum (#630697)
- 1 sheet floral pattern (#633384)
- 2 sheets block pattern (#635067)

Materials:
- Floral stickers (#554481)
- Pink ribbon

Page 23
ASHFORD LAMP SHADE
designed by Pamela Lange
Papers:
- 3 sheets olive floral pattern (#634411)

(continued on next page)

(continued from previous page)

Materials:
- Lamp shade
- Purple ribbon

Page 23
ASHFORD FLORAL CARD
designed by Sue Elred
Papers:
- 1 sheet olive cardstock (#630963)
- 1 sheet olive floral pattern (#634411)
- 1 sheet tan pattern (#633926)
Materials:
- Floral borders (#552821)
- Journal tags (#552838)

Page 24
ALL BOY MINI ALBUM
designed by Ruth Giauque
Paper:
- 1 sheet blue cardstock (#631083)

Materials:
- 3 buttons
- 6"x6" album (#535138)
- Manila tag
- Silver star brad
- Stick
- Toy stickers (#554641)
- Twine

Page 25
CLASSIC
designed by Jenni Bowlin

Papers:
- 1 sheet blue plaid pattern (#633605)
- 1 sheet copper foil paper
- 1 sheet ivory cardstock (#630918)
- 1 sheet red linen pattern (#633612)
- 1 sheet stripe pattern (#633759)
- 1 sheet toy pattern (#633636)
Materials:
- Embellishments
- Manila tags
- Toy alphabet stickers (#223004)
- Toy stickers (#552463)

Page 26
RODEO DAYS
designed by Pamela Lange
Papers:
- 1 sheet bandana pattern (#636644)
- 1 sheet brown cowboy pattern (#636705)
- 1 sheet cowboy images pattern (#554856)
- 1 sheet cowboy pattern (#636606)
- 1 sheet cowhide pattern (#636712)
- 1 sheet denim pattern (#636668)
- 1 sheet plaid pattern (#636682)
- 1 sheet red gingham pattern (#636699)
- 1 sheet stripe pattern (#636651)
Materials:
- Manila tags
- Twine

Page 27
HOWDY PARTNER CARD AND ENVELOPE
designed by Cary Oliver
Papers:
- 1 sheet cowhide pattern (#636712)
- 1 sheet denim pattern (#636675)
Materials:
- Copper brads
- Cowboy images sticker (#551534)
- Gray legal envelope
- Leather strips

Page 27
BANDANA FOLD-A-NOTE
designed by Cary Oliver
Papers:
- 2 sheets bandana pattern (#636644)
Materials:
- Leather strips
- Silver concha

Page 27
COWBOY MINI ALBUM AND TAG
designed by Cary Oliver
Papers:
- 1 sheet bandana pattern (#636644)
- 1 sheet cowhide pattern (#636712)
Materials:
- Leather strips
- Mini album with photograph frame
- Silver brads

Page 27
LASSO THE MOON
designed by Cary Oliver

Papers:
- 1 sheet beige cowboy pattern (#636705)
- 1 sheet brown suede pattern (#631205)
- 1 sheet ivory cardstock (#630918)

Materials:
- Leather strips
- Silver concha

Page 28
ZAC
designed by Twyla Koop

Papers:
- 1 sheet blue plaid pattern (#633605)
- 1 sheet brown cardstock
- 1 sheet marching toys pattern (#633636)
- 1 sheet red linen pattern (#633612)

Materials:
- Antique toy stickers (#552456)
- Fibers
- Gold brads
- Gold grommets
- Toy alphabet stickers (#223004)

Page 29
LOVE OF THE GAME
designed by Leslie Wilson

Papers:
- 1 sheet brown cardstock
- 1 sheet ivory cardstock (#630918)
- 2 sheets beige cardstock

- 2 sheets tan leather pattern (#620162)

Materials:
- Brown embroidery floss
- Brown eyelets
- Leather strips

Page 29
TODAY IS A GIFT
designed by Rebecca Robinson

Papers:
- 1 sheet botanical pattern (#632677)
- 1 sheet bronze cardstock (#630956)
- 1 sheet parchment green pattern (#632752)
- 1 sheet red linen pattern (#633612)
- 1 sheet Toscana pattern (#632561)

Materials:
- Fibers
- Floral photo corner stickers (#551381)
- Manila tags

Page 30
BLUE JOURNAL
designed by Pamela Lange

Papers:
- 2 sheets blue dot pattern (#610729)

Materials:
- Cream ribbon
- Fibers
- Journal
- Vintage charms (#558786)

Page 31
INQUIRE WITHIN
designed by Ruth Giauque

Papers:
- 1 sheet blue cardstock (#631083)
- 1 sheet blue floral fabric pattern (#610484)
- 1 sheet ivory cardstock (#630918)
- 1 sheet large floral fabric pattern (#610378)
- 1 sheet navy cardstock (#630970)
- 1 sheet tan linen pattern (#633926)

Materials:
- Blue gingham ribbon
- Blue ribbon
- Brass metal label holder
- Fibers
- Manila tag
- Miniature fabric flower
- Silver button

Pages 32–33
OLIVIA'S GARDEN
designed by Brenda Walton

Papers:
- 1 sheet clear vellum (#630697)
- 1 sheet dot paper pattern (#633209)
- 1 sheet floral pattern (#636026)

(continued on next page)

(continued from previous page)

- 1 sheet floral pattern (#636088)
- 1 sheet gingham pattern (#633247)
- 1 sheet ivory pattern (#633513)
- 1 sheet mint dot pattern (#633858)
- 1 sheet pearlessence pattern (#633339)
- 1 sheet pink pattern (#633322)
- 1 sheet rose vellum (#633216)
- 1 sheet white cardstock (#630901)
- 2 sheets rose paper pattern (#633209)

Materials:
- Rose alphabet (#553026)
- Rose border stickers (#552555)
- Rose journal tags (#552470)
- Rose stickers (#552494)

Page 32
PINK FLORAL CARD
designed by Pamela Lange
Papers:
- 1 sheet clear vellum (#630697)
- 1 sheet pink floral pattern (#636026)
- 1 sheet white cardstock (#630902)

Page 33
ADDRESS BOOK
designed by Ruth Giauque
Paper:
- Ivory cardstock (#630918)

Materials:
- 6"x6" album (#535121)
- Assorted stickers (#554689, #554658, #554672, #554146)

Page 34
COLLAGE FRAME
designed by Ruth Giauque
Papers:
- 1 sheet floral pattern (#635548)
- 1 sheet olive floral pattern (#635555)
- 1 sheet script pattern (#635975)
- 1 sheet stripe pattern (#635531)
- 1 sheet quilt pattern (#635067)

Materials:
- 6"x6" wooden frame
- Assorted buttons
- Green gingham ribbon
- Key
- Lock

Page 35
CHERISHED FAMILY
designed by Debbie Turner
Papers:
- 1 sheet floral stripe pattern (#635500)
- 1 sheet olive cardstock (#630963)
- 1 sheet olive floral pattern (#634411)
- 1 sheet olive floral vellum (#634428)
- 1 sheet ribbon pattern (#635517)
- 1 sheet sage cardstock (#630925)
- 1 sheet stripe pattern (#635531)

Materials:
- Flower stickers (#554450)
- Sheer white ribbon

Page 36
GRANDMA'S ROSE GARDEN
designed by Patricia Gutierrez
Papers:
- 1 sheet floral pearlessence pattern (#633339)
- 1 sheet ivory cardstock (#630918)
- 1 sheet olive cardstock (#630963)
- 1 sheet rose pattern (#633186)

Materials:
- Floral stickers (#552401)

Page 37
TO BE YOURSELF
designed by Jennifer Ditterich
Papers:
- 1 sheet cream vellum (#630697)
- 1 sheet peach block pattern (#638082)
- 1 sheet peach plaid pattern (#637719)

Materials:
- Floral sticker (#554054)
- Green ribbon
- Peach ribbon

Page 38
BELLA CARD HOLDER
designed by Pamela Lange

(continued to next page)

(continued from previous page)

Paper:
- 1 sheet acorn pattern (#634510)

Materials:
- Postage stamp sticker (#554184)

Page 39
1912
designed by Brenda Walton

Papers:
- 1 sheet botanical pattern (#635265)
- 1 sheet die-cut pattern (#651128)
- 1 sheet floral border pattern (#635296)
- 1 sheet folk art pattern (#634541)
- 1 sheet lavender pattern (#634534)
- 1 sheet small diamond pattern (#634558)

Materials:
- Assorted buttons
- Decorative tack
- Die-cut alphabet stickers (#553064)
- Green ribbon

Page 40
BELLA MEMORIES
designed by Brenda Walton

Papers:
- 1 sheet botanical pattern (#634398)
- 1 sheet lavender pattern (#634510)
- 1 sheet plum and olive diamond pattern (#634572)
- 2 sheets folk art pattern (#634541)

Materials:
- Blue gingham ribbon
- Border stickers (#551527)
- Botanical banner sticker (#554719)
- Botanical journal tags (#552739)
- Cord
- Decorative tack
- Floral corner stickers (#554740)
- Floral stickers (#552777)
- Gold sequins

Page 41
BELLA FAN
designed by Kelly Keller

Papers:
- 1 sheet botanical pattern (#634398)
- 1 sheet clear vellum (#630697)

Materials:
- Gold ribbon
- Fan

Page 42
DEAR FRIEND
designed by Brenda Walton

Papers:
- 1 sheet border pattern (#633087)
- 1 sheet die-cut pattern (#651067)
- 1 sheet lilac vellum (#633056)
- 1 sheet pearlessence vellum (#633841)
- 1 sheet small floral pattern (#633094)
- 2 sheets lavender block pattern (#633070)

- 2 sheets light lavender pattern (#633315)

Materials:
- Pearl buttons
- Pink variegated ribbon
- Ribbon
- Velvet flowers and leaves

Page 43
JULIANA GIFT BOX
designed by Pamela Lange

Papers:
- 2 sheets lavender damask pattern (#634169)

Materials:
- Lavender medallion stickers (#554023)
- Purple Ribbon

Page 43
JULIANA STATIONERY
designed by Ruth Giauque

Papers:
- 1 sheet lavender blocks pattern (#633070)
- 1 sheet lavender floral print pattern (#633094)

Materials:
- Dragonfly and flower stickers (#554016)

Page 43
LOVE
designed by Kelly Keller

Papers:
- 1 sheet clear vellum (#630697)
- 1 sheet lavender block pattern (#633070)

(continued to next page)

(continued from previous page)

- 1 sheet lavender floral vellum (#633056)
- 1 sheet lavender suede pattern (#633834)
- 2 sheets lavender floral pattern (#633049)

Materials:
- Beads
- Lavender corner stickers (#552517)
- Lavender journal tags (#552562)
- Purple ribbons
- Silver clip

Pages 44–45
THERE'S NO PLACE LIKE HOME
designed by Brenda Walton

Papers:
- 1 sheet Brianna bird pattern (#639003)
- 1 sheet diamond and stripe pattern (#638778)
- 1 sheet flocked gold pattern (#637399)
- 1 sheet ivory cardstock (#630918)
- 2 sheets large flower pattern (#637030)
- 2 sheets vine flower pattern (#638785)

Materials:
- Amelia border stickers (#551497)
- Gold eyelets
- Journal tags (#551909)

Page 46
SEASHORE MEMORIES JOURNAL
designed by Kelly Keller

Papers:
- 1 sheet berry floral pattern (#634213)
- 1 sheet clear vellum (#630697)
- 1 sheet small dot pattern (#633261)
- 2 sheets aqua plaid pattern (#634497)

Materials:
- Boat stickers (#554245)
- Fibers
- Green beads
- Miniature bottle
- Sea stickers (#554108)
- White eyelets

Page 47
NEW ZEALAND WEDDING
designed by Brenda Walton

Papers:
- 1 sheet ivory cardstock (#630918)
- 1 sheet lavender swirl glitter pattern (#636187)
- 1 sheet light green cardstock (#631021)
- 1 sheet olive cardstock (#630963)
- 1 sheet pink cardstock (#631014)
- 2 sheets rose bouquet pattern (#636132)

Materials:
- Clear glitter
- Domed words (#557260)
- Floral corner stickers (#551596)
- Floral vine borders (#551619)

- Friendship tags (#555419)
- Green ribbon

Page 47
SOMERSET SHADOW BOX
designed by Brenda Walton

Papers:
- 1 sheet lavender swirls pattern (#636002)
- 1 sheet light green cardstock (#631021)
- 1 sheet roses and vine pattern (#638754)

Materials:
- Floral corner stickers (#551596)
- Gold ring
- Purple ribbon
- Resin butterfly (#559271)

Tim Coffey

Page 48
BEST WISHES CARD
designed by Pamela Lange

Papers:
- 1 sheet light green cardstock (#631021)
- 1 sheet yellow vine pattern (#634770)

Materials:
- Butterfly stickers (#554320)
- Die-cut alphabet stickers (#553040)

Page 49
DREAMING OF DAFFODILS
designed by Kay Stanley

(continued to next page)

(continued from previous page)

Papers:
- 3 sheets floral pattern (#637269)

Materials:
- Daffodil frame sticker (#555297)

Page 50
BLOSSOM
designed by Jennifer Ditterich

Papers:
- 1 sheet clear vellum (#630697)
- 1 sheet lavender stripe pattern (#635081)
- 2 sheets plaid pattern (#634473)
- 2 sheets poppy pattern (#635173)

Materials:
- Green ribbon
- Lavender embroidery floss
- Silver brads
- Silver eyelets

Page 51
BLUE POPPY CARD
designed by Pamela Lange

Papers:
- 1 sheet lavender stripe pattern (#635081)
- 1 sheet plaid pattern (#635951)
- 1 sheet white cardstock (#630901)

Materials:
- Flower sticker (#554382)
- Lavender border sticker (#553517)

Page 52
DAISY BIRTHDAY CAKE
designed by Pamela Lange

Papers:
- 1 sheet daisy glitter vellum (#635807)

- 3 sheets daisy pattern (#634749)
- 11 sheets daisy ivory pattern (#635845)

Materials:
- White ribbon
- Yellow ribbon

Page 53
DAISY CROWN
designed by Pamela Lange

Papers:
- 1 sheet daisy glitter pattern (#635791)
- 1 sheet daisy pattern (#634749)

Materials:
- Green floral tape
- Green gingham ribbon
- String of pearls
- White ribbon
- White toile
- Yellow ribbon

Page 53
DAISY INVITATION AND ENVELOPE
designed by Pamela Lange

Papers:
- 1 sheet daisy pattern (#634763)
- 1 sheet daisy vellum (#634756)
- 1 sheet green gingham pattern (#635814)
- 1 sheet yellow gingham pattern (#635128)

Materials:
- Die-cut alphabet stickers (#553040)
- Silver glitter

Page 53
DAISY PINWHEEL
designed by Kelly Keller

Papers:
- 4 sheets daisy pattern (#634749)

Materials:
- 18" dowel
- Butterfly stickers (#554320)
- Nail
- Silver glitter

Page 54
DAISY DELIGHT
designed by Kelly Keller

Papers:
- 1 sheet clear vellum (#630697)
- 1 sheet daisy vellum (#634756)
- 1 sheet vine pattern (#634770)
- 1 sheet white cardstock (#630901)
- 1 sheet yellow gingham pattern (#635128)
- 2 sheets daisy pattern (#634749)

Materials:
- Silver eyelets
- Yellow ribbon

Page 55
HAPPY BIRTHDAY CARD
designed by Pamela Lange

Papers:
- 1 sheet daisy pattern (#634763)
- 1 sheet ivory cardstock (#630918)
- 1 sheet yellow gingham pattern (#635128)

(continued to next page)

(continued from previous page)

Materials:
- Daisy resin frame sticker (#559301)
- Daisy resin sticker (#559325)

Page 56

DAISY CANDLELIGHT
designed by Pamela Lange

Papers:
- 1 sheet daisy pattern (#634763)
- 1 sheet green vellum (#630727)

Materials:
- Candlelight with shade
- Daisy stickers (#552883)

Page 56

ALL OCCASION CARD
designed by Pamela Lange

Papers:
- 1 sheet butterfly pattern (#637979)
- 1 sheet ivory cardstock (#630918)
- 1 sheet lavender stencil pattern (#637061)
- 2 sheets lavender diamond pattern (#637993)

Materials:
- Purple ribbon

Page 57

AS TIME GOES BY
designed by Jennifer Ditterich

Papers:
- 1 sheet floral stamp pattern (#636941)
- 1 sheet lavender stencil pattern (#637061)

Materials:
- Brown buttons
- Gold mat board
- Gold ribbon
- Metal collage frame (#558694)

Page 58

FRIENDS
designed by Jennifer Ditterich

Papers:
- 1 sheet lavender botanical pattern (#636910)
- 1 sheet lavender stencil pattern (#637061)

Materials:
- Butterfly stickers (#551848)
- Fibers
- Green gem
- Manila tag
- Purple ribbon

Page 59

LE FLEUR PURSE
designed by Pamela Lange

Papers:
- 1 sheet floral stamp pattern (#636941)
- 2 sheets lavender stencil pattern (#637061)

Materials:
- Assorted rhinestones
- Cigar box
- Clear domed stickers (#557420)
- Fibers

- Hydrangea border stickers (#551893)
- Purple cord
- Purple ribbon
- Ribbon flowers
- White lace

Page 59

MINI PHONE BOOK AND TAG
designed by Pamela Lange

Papers:
- 1 sheet ivory cardstock (#630918)
- 1 sheet lavender stencil pattern (#637061)
- 1 sheet lavender stripe pattern (#637931)
- 1 sheet purple butterfly pattern (#636835)

Materials:
- 2 binding discs
- Assorted beads
- Butterfly stickers (#551848)
- Chipboard
- Fibers
- Journal tags (#551862)
- Manila tag

Page 60

'TIS THE SEASON CHRISTMAS CARDS
Red Poinsettia designed by Jennifer Ditterich

Papers:
- 1 sheet holiday pattern (#637207)
- 1 sheet holiday stripe pattern (#637160)

(continued to next page)

(continued from previous page)

Materials:
- Fibers
- Holiday flower stickers (#551800)

White Poinsettia designed by Pamela Lange
Papers:
- 1 sheet green damask pattern (#637108)
- 1 sheet holiday pattern (#637207)

Materials:
- Assorted ribbon
- Holiday flower stickers (#551800)

Page 61
NOEL
designed by Jennifer Ditterich
Papers:
- 1 sheet holiday stripe pattern (#637160)
- 1 sheet red cardstock (#631045)
- 2 sheets holiday pattern (#637207)

Materials:
- Holiday journal tags (#551824)
- Red ribbon

Page 62
KAELA
designed by Kelly Keller
Papers:
- 1 sheet ivory cardstock (#630918)
- 1 sheet lavender stripe pattern (#637931)
- 2 sheets pressed flower pattern (#636781)
- 2 sheets lavender stencil pattern (#637061)

Materials:
- Butterfly stickers (#551848)
- Cream buttons
- Fibers
- Green ribbon
- Leaves

Page 63
TRIPLE GIFT PACK
designed by Pamela Lange
Papers:
- 2 sheets damask pattern (#637108)

Materials:
- Floral border stickers (#551893)
- Gold ribbon

Page 63
EMBELLISHED STRIPED FRAME
designed by Pamela Lange
Paper:
- 1 sheet striped pattern (#637818)

Materials:
- Cream ribbon
- Frame

Page 64
ISABELLA CARDS
designed by Tamara Gilchrist
(card on the right)
Papers:
- 1 sheet ivory cardstock (#630918)
- 1 sheet ivory suede pattern (#634374)

Materials:
- Journal tag sticker (#552838)
- White beads

(card on the left)
Papers:
- 1 sheet clear vellum (#630697)
- 1 sheet green pattern (#635524)
- 1 sheet script pattern (#635975)

Materials:
- Gold brads
- Flower sticker (#552814)

Page 65
PRINCESS ANA MARIA
designed by Patricia Gutierrez
Papers:
- 1 sheet stripe pattern (#635531)
- 1 sheet toile pattern (#635494)

Materials:
- 3 sheets floral stickers (#554450)
- Family names stickers (#554405)
- Heart-shaped button
- Sheer white ribbon

Page 66
ISABELLA ALTERED ALBUM
designed by Pamela Lange
Materials:
- Album (#535046)
- Assorted buttons
- White lace

Page 66
ISABELLA TREASURE BOX
designed by Pamela Lange
Papers:
- 2 sheets floral pattern (#634459)

(continued to next page)

(continued from previous page)

Materials:
- Papier-mâché box
- Gold ribbon

Pages 66–67
REMEMBER WHEN
designed by Jennifer Ditterich
Papers:
- 1 sheet floral pattern (#634459)
- 1 sheet ribbon pattern (#635517)
- 2 sheets toile pattern (#635494)

Materials:
- Family name stickers (#554405)
- Journal tags (#552838)
- Olive floral borders and corner stickers (#552821)
- White ribbon

Pages 68–69
HERITAGE ALTERED FRAME
designed by Pamela Lange
Paper:
- 1 sheet black stripe pattern (#633759)

Materials:
- Green gingham ribbon
- Metal art frame (#558014)

Pages 68–69
HERITAGE HATBOXES
designed by Pamela Lange
Papers:
- 1 sheet brown pattern (#633704)
- 1 sheet French wallpaper pattern (#635944)
- 1 sheet stripe pattern (#633735)
- 2 sheets black stripe pattern (#633759)

- 2 sheets forest gingham pattern (#635623)
- 2 sheets fruit pattern (#633650)
- 3 sheets brick red diamond pattern (#633674)
- 3 sheets green plaid pattern (#633667)
- 4 sheets burgundy plaid pattern (#634077)
- 4 sheets heritage pattern (#633728)

Materials:
- Assorted cord
- Assorted fringe
- Assorted ribbon
- Assorted tassels
- Cream buttons
- Hatboxes

Page 70
GRANDMA'S ATTIC
designed by Jennifer Ditterich
Papers:
- 1 sheet cream vellum (#630703)
- 1 sheet floral pattern (#635548)
- 1 sheet ivory quilt pattern (#635043)
- 1 sheet olive floral pattern (#634411)
- 1 sheet olive floral vellum (#634428)
- 2 sheets floral stripe pattern (#635500)

Materials:
- Green ribbon
- Pink embroidery floss

Page 71
LETTER FROM THE PAST
designed by Kelley Brewington
Papers:
- 1 sheet accent pattern (#633407)
- 1 sheet floral border pattern (#633919)
- 1 sheet green parchment pattern (#632752)
- 1 sheet ivory cardstock (#630918)
- 1 sheet tan parchment pattern (#632769)
- 2 sheets floral pattern (#633384)

Materials:
- Family name stickers (#554405)
- Journal tag stickers (#552661)

Page 71
WEDDING TAG
designed by Pamela Lange
Papers:
- 1 sheet clear vellum (#630697)
- 1 sheet floral pattern (#633384)

Materials:
- Fibers
- Floral frames stickers (#554474)
- Pink ribbon

Page 71
ASHFORD BOX
designed by Sue Elred
Paper:
- 1 sheet floral pattern (#633384)
Materials:
- Floral border sticker (#552609)
- Floral sticker (#552647)

(continued to next page)

(continued to next page)

(continued from previous page)

- 2 sheets Florence glitter pattern (#636057)
- 2 sheets white shimmer fabric patterns (#610002)

Materials:
- 2 sheets border stickers (#552968)
- Frames and tags stickers (#554139)
- Gold rings
- Pearls
- Pink ribbon
- Rose large frames stickers (#554221)
- Rose stickers (#554214)

Page 79
FLOWERS FOR YOU
designed by Pamela Lange
Papers:
- 1 sheet bouquet stripes pattern (#636033)
- 1 sheet ivory cardstock (#630918)

Materials:
- Flower resin stickers (#559554)
- Ribbon

Page 80
WEDDING INVITATION
designed by Patricia Gutierrez
Paper:
- 1 sheet floral embossed pattern (#633889)

Materials:
- Flower border stickers (#554627)
- Flower stickers (#554603)

- Papier-mâché heart
- White braid
- White ribbon

Page 81
LACE-TRIMMED CARD AND TAG
designed by Patricia Guterriez
Papers:
- 1 sheet pearl vellum (#630567)
- 1 sheet white cardstock (#630901)

Materials:
- Flower border stickers (#554627)
- Flower stickers (#554603)
- White doily
- White ribbon

Page 81
WEDDING DAY PICTURE
designed by Patricia Gutierrez
Paper:
- 1 sheet floral embossed pattern (#633889)

Materials:
- Cream braid
- Gold thread
- Papier-mâché heart
- Wedding stickers (#554504)

Page 82
GIFT CARDS AND ENVELOPE
designed by Pamela Lange
(top card)
Papers:
- 1 sheet bouquet glitter pattern (#636040)
- 1 sheet ivory cardstock (#630918)

Materials:
- Border sticker (#552517)

- Cream ribbon
- Domed alphabet stickers (#557345)
- Flower sticker (#554221)

(bottom card)
Papers:
- 1 sheet floral glitter pattern (#636026)
- 1 sheet white cardstock (#630901)

Materials:
- Pink ribbon
- Wedding ribbon sticker (#554504)

Page 83
(top card)
Papers:
- 1 sheet floral glitter pattern (#636064)
- 1 sheet light green cardstock (#631021)

Materials:
- Border stickers (#552449)
- Ribbon
- Season stickers (#552760)

(bottom card)
Papers:
- 1 sheet floral glitter pattern (#636064)
- 1 sheet ivory cardstock (#630918)

Materials:
- Floral sticker (#554146)
- Garden border stickers (#552913)

Page 84
TO LOVE, HONOR, AND CHERISH
designed by Lori Bergman

(continued to next page)

(continued from previous page)

Papers:

- 1 sheet bouquet glitter vellum (#636095)
- 1 sheet clear vellum (#630697)
- 1 sheet white shimmer fabric pattern (#610002)

Materials:

- Domed typewriter key stickers (#557031)
- Floral corner stickers (#551336)
- Ivory accordion book (#536296)
- Silver brads
- Wedding stickers (#554504)

Page 85
ALTERED WEDDING ALBUM
designed by Pamela Lange
Paper:

- 1 sheet floral stripe pattern (#635500)

Materials:

- 6"x6" floral album (#534049)
- Cream ribbon

Page 86
HUMPTY DUMPTY CARD
designed by Pamela Lange
Papers:

- 1 sheet green vellum (#630727)
- 1 sheet ivory cardstock (#630918)
- 1 sheet plaid pattern (#632578)

Materials:

- Storytime stickers (#554429)

Page 87
BABY JACK
designed by Kay Stanley
Papers:

- 1 sheet clear vellum (#630697)
- 2 sheets cuddly friends border pattern (#633995)

Materials:

- Blue ribbon
- White buttons

Page 88
MY FIRST BOOK
designed by Pamela Lange
Papers:

- 1 sheet blue stripe pattern (#633940)
- 1 sheet hearts border pattern (#635388)
- 1 sheet pink cardstock (#631014)
- 1 sheet pink dot pattern (#633957)
- 1 sheet pink gingham pattern (#633247)
- 1 sheet white cardstock (#630901)

Materials:

- Assorted buttons
- Assorted eyelets
- Cuddly friends border stickers (#552531)
- Cuddly friends stickers (#554580)
- Ivory accordion book (#536296)
- Ivory ribbon

Page 88
BABY LAMP
designed by Pamela Lange
Papers:

- 1 sheet blocked pattern (#635180)
- 2 sheets rolling hills with sheep pattern (#635203)

Materials:

- Cylinder lamp

Page 89
FIELD OF DREAMS
designed by Pamela Lange
Papers:

- 1 sheet clear vellum (#630697)
- 1 sheet yellow gingham pattern (#635128)
- 3 sheets rolling hills pattern (#635203)
- 3 sheets rolling hills with sheep pattern (#635197)

Materials:

- 3 journal tag stickers (#552906)
- Fibers
- Purple embroidery floss
- White ribbon

Pages 90–91
OUR SWEET GRANDBABY
designed by Kay Stanley
Papers:

- 1 sheet clear vellum (#630727)
- 1 sheet floral borders (#561380)
- 1 sheet green vellum (#630727)
- 1 sheet ivory cardstock (#630918)
- 1 sheet yellow flower pattern (#632066)

(continued to next page)

(continued from previous page)

- 2 sheets ivory floral embossed pattern (#630086)
- 2 sheets plaid pattern (#632578)

Materials:
- Lace border stickers (#561380)
- Lace corner stickers (#551381)

Page 92
NOTES OF LOVE
designed by Kelly Keller

Papers:
- 1 sheet blue stripe pattern (#633940)
- 1 sheet cuddly friends pattern (#633445)
- 1 sheet cuddly friends pattern vellum (#633452)
- 1 sheet pink dot pattern (#633957)
- 1 sheet yellow stripe pattern (#633964)
- 2 sheets white cardstock (#630901)

Materials:
- Cream buttons
- Cuddly friends border stickers (#552531)
- Cuddly friends stickers (#552425)
- White rickrack

Page 93
BABY BOY CARD
designed by Pamela Lange

Papers:
- 1 sheet blue cardstock (#631083)
- 1 sheet chenille stripe pattern (#633940)

- 1 sheet die-cut pattern (#651074)
- 1 sheet white cardstock (#630901)

Materials:
- Green border stickers (#552548)

Page 94
FOREST JOURNAL
designed by Pamela Lange

Papers:
- 1 sheet brown leather pattern (#620056)
- 1 sheet forest sculpture pattern (#610668)

Materials:
- Green gingham ribbon
- Metal lock and key charms (#558373)
- Small notebook

Page 95
MY BEST FRIEND
designed by Debbie Turner

Papers:
- 1 sheet antique fabric pattern (#610446)
- 1 sheet chestnut pattern (#635739)
- 1 sheet hunting pattern (#634893)
- 1 sheet hunting pattern vellum (#634909)
- 1 sheet tan leather pattern (#620162)

Materials:
- Hunting sticker (#554252)

Page 96–97
MY HERO *(two pages)*
designed by Debbie Turner

Papers:
- 1 sheet green plaid pattern vellum (#634961)
- 1 sheet nature pattern (#635593)
- 1 sheet red plaid pattern vellum (#634930)
- 2 sheets chestnut pattern (#635739)
- 2 sheets red plaid pattern (#634923)

Materials:
- Fibers
- Tags

Page 98
WILLIAM "PETE" ROGERS
designed by Pamela Lange

Papers:
- 1 sheet green script pattern (#638396)
- 1 sheet red pattern (#633612)
- 1 sheet vintage flag pattern (#638228)
- 2 sheets camouflage pattern (#638273)
- 2 sheets wartime memories pattern (#638259)

Materials:
- American flag stickers (#555051)
- Army stickers (#555006)
- Green cord
- Mahogany Frame (#391062)
- Patriotic frame stickers (#555068)

(continued to next page)

(continued from previous page)

Papers:

- 1 sheet ivory cardstock (#630918)
- 1 sheet ledger pattern (#636361)
- 1 sheet map pattern (#636767)
- 1 sheet postcards pattern (#636262)
- 1 sheet rust cardstock (#630956)

Materials:

- Black label stickers (#551756)
- Domed random reversed alphabet stickers (#557116)
- Domed watches (#557062)
- Domed wood block alphabet (#557598)
- Embellishments
- Fibers
- Large gated kraft ring-bound book (#536364)
- Metal art word plates (#558045)
- Metal frames (#558007)
- Paper clip
- Tag
- Twine

Page 104
ALTERED SEWING FORM
designed by Holly Nelsen
Papers:

- 1 sheet black stripe pattern (#633759)
- 1 sheet dictionary pattern (#636279)
- 1 sheet furniture pattern (#636477)
- 1 sheet toile pattern (#633742)

Materials:

- Assorted buttons
- Assorted ribbon
- Domed black typewriter key stickers (#557031)
- Domed frames (#557000)
- Domed random alphabet stickers (#557109)
- Domed random reversed alphabet stickers (#557116)
- Domed stamp stickers (#557024)
- Embellishments
- Fibers
- Metal brass alphabet (#558076)
- Metal word plates (#558046)
- Papier-mâché sewing form
- Tape measure
- Word stickers (#554795)

Page 105
BITS AND PIECES
designed by Tracey Niehues
Papers:

- 1 sheet button pattern vellum (#636422)
- 1 sheet dictionary pattern (#636279)
- 1 sheet flowers and letters pattern (#636200)
- 1 sheet ivory cardstock (#630918)
- 1 sheet metal art frames pattern (#558014)
- 1 sheet pink tissue paper

Materials:

- Buggy tag stickers (#551558)

- Domed Goudy alphabet stickers (#557048)
- Domed scissors (#557017)
- Domed random reversed alphabet stickers (#557116)
- Domed white typewriter key stickers (#557055)
- Fibers
- Metal brass alphabet stickers (#558076)
- Metal frames (#558007)
- Pink ribbon
- Puzzle pieces

Page 106
MY GRANDMOTHER
designed by Tracey Niehues
Papers:

- 1 sheet black cardstock (#631007)
- 1 sheet furniture pattern (#636453)
- 1 sheet map pattern (#636330)
- 1 sheet postcards pattern (#636262)
- 1 sheet script pattern (#636378)
- 2 sheets light blue cardstock (#631038)
- 2 sheets Norfolk rose indigo fabric pattern (#610378)

Materials:

- Assorted buttons
- Domed black typewriter key stickers (#557031)
- Domed Goudy alphabet stickers (#557048)

(continued to next page)

(continued from previous page)

- Embellishments
- Gold tassel
- Manila tag

Page 107
PHOTO FILE
designed by Tracey Niehues
Papers:

- 1 sheet blocher pattern (#636477)
- 1 sheet dark brown leather fabric pattern (#620056)
- 1 sheet dictionary pattern (#636279)
- 1 sheet ivory cardstock (#630918)
- 1 sheet ledger pattern (#636361)
- 1 sheet script pattern (#636378)
- 1 sheet white shimmer fabric pattern (#610002)

Materials:

- Canceled-check file folder
- Domed Goudy alphabet stickers (#557048)
- Domed random reversed alphabet stickers (#557116)
- Embellishments
- Fibers
- Nail heads
- Shipping tags

Page 108
GENERATIONS
designed by Tracey Niehues
Papers:

- 1 sheet furniture pattern (#636460)
- 1 sheet ivory cardstock (#630918)

- 1 sheet script and buttons pattern (#636538)
- 1 sheet white shimmer fabric pattern (#610002)

Materials:

- Always tag sticker (#551541)
- Button frame sticker (#554818)
- Buttons
- Domed black typewriter key stickers (#557031)
- Domed random reversed alphabet stickers (#557116)
- Gold ribbon

Page 109
WINDOW OF THE SOUL ACCORDION BOOK
designed by Tracey Niehues
Papers:

- 1 sheet dictionary pattern (#636279)
- 1 sheet newspaper pattern (#636477)
- 1 sheet quotes pattern (#636521)
- 1 sheet script pattern (#636378)

Materials:

- Domed frame stickers (#557000)

Page 109
PURSE
designed by Tracey Niehues
Papers:

- 1 sheet dictionary pattern (#636279)
- 1 sheet flowers and letters pattern (#636200)
- 1 sheet olive check fabric pattern

(#610347)

Materials:

- Binding disc
- Decorative button
- Domed black typewriter key stickers (#557031)
- Fibers
- Gold chain
- Gold tassel
- Metal art frames (#558007)

Page 109
DOMINO TAG BOOK
designed by Tracey Niehues
Papers:

- 1 sheet dictionary pattern (#636279)
- 1 sheet map pattern (#636330)

Materials:

- Cream buttons
- Domed domino stickers (#557635)
- Fabric scrap
- Fibers
- Frames and stamps stickers (#554771)
- Ivory tag book (#536777)
- Measurement stickers (#551565)
- Nickel buttons (#563070)
- Tag

Pages 110–111
GREAT, GREAT, GREAT-GRANDFATHER BURNSIDE
designed by Cary Oliver

(continued to next page)

(continued from previous page)

Papers:
- 1 sheet black cardstock (#631007)
- 1 sheet dictionary pattern (#636279)
- 2 sheets furniture newspaper pattern (#636453)
- 2 sheets ivory cardstock (#630918)

Materials:
- Decorative tacks (#563001)
- Domed scissors and tag stickers (#557017)
- Domed stamp stickers (#557024)
- Metal alphabet pieces (#558076)
- Metal frames (#558007)
- Red ribbon

Page 112
RULER JOURNAL
designed by Melanie Cantrell

Papers:
- 1 sheet postcard pattern (#636262)
- 1 sheet script pattern (#636293)
- 1 sheet tape measure pattern (#636552)

Materials:
- Always tag sticker (#551541)
- Blue gingham ribbon
- Ledger
- Metal tag (#558038)
- Rose sticker (#552401)

Page 112
THE TOUR
designed by Pamela Lange

Papers:
- 1 sheet newspaper pattern (#636477)
- 1 sheet postcard pattern (#638433)
- 1 sheet quotes overlay pattern (#636514)

Materials:
- Assorted ribbon
- Kraft mini paper bag
- Manila tag

Page 112
QUILT MEMORIES
designed by Pamela Lange

Papers:
- 1 sheet gingham pattern (#638488)
- 1 sheet ivory cardstock (#630918)
- 1 sheet quilt pattern (#638464)

Materials:
- Assorted buttons
- Rectangle metal frame (#563452)
- White Lace

Page 113
ALTERED BOXES
designed by Pamela Lange

Papers:
- 1 sheet dictionary pattern (#636279)
- 1 sheet flower pattern (#636200)
- 1 sheet music pattern (#636286)
- 2 sheets pansy pattern (#636408)

Materials:
- 3 papier-mâché boxes
- Clear domed stickers (#557420)
- Manila tag
- Purple ribbon

Page 114–115
SOMETHING OLD, SOMETHING NEW
designed by Melanie Cantrell, Pamela Lange, and Tracey Niehues

Papers:
- 1 sheet map pattern (#636767)
- 1 sheet newspaper pattern (#636477)
- 1 sheet postcards pattern (#636736)
- 1 sheet quilt pattern (#635067)
- 1 sheet quotes pattern (#636521)
- 1 sheet tan leather pattern (#620025)
- 1 sheet wood tape measure pattern (#636552)

Materials:
- Assorted brads
- Assorted buttons
- Assorted ribbons
- Domed frame stickers (#557000)
- Domed random alphabet stickers (#557116)
- Manila tags
- Stamp stickers (#551688)
- White lace
- Wood tape measure stickers (#551565)
- Word stickers (#554795)

Page 116
CHRISTMAS CARD
designed by Melanie Cantrell
Papers:
- 1 sheet holly vine pattern (#634800)
- 1 sheet ivory cardstock (#630918)
- 1 sheet red vine pattern (#635876)

Materials:
- Buttons
- Christmas stickers (#554290)
- Ribbon

Page 117
CHRISTMAS GARLAND
designed by Kay Stanley
Papers:
- 1 sheet floral pattern (#635524)
- 1 sheet floral pattern (#635548)
- 1 sheet floral stripe pattern (#635500)
- 1 sheet linen pattern (#635524)
- 1 sheet Louisiana pattern (#636750)
- 1 sheet red gingham pattern (#636699)
- 1 sheet ribbon pattern (#635517)
- 1 sheet script pattern (#636975)
- 1 sheet swirl pattern (#632653)

Materials:
- Accent border sticker (#552685)

- Cream buttons
- Floral border stickers (#551527, #552791, #552821)
- Gold ribbon
- Gold string
- Red cord
- Red tassels
- White lace

Page 118
ADVENT WREATH
designed by Lori Bergman
Papers:
- 1 sheet red vine pattern (#635876)
- 2 sheets green starlight pattern (#635098)
- 2 sheets red diamond pattern (#635104)
- 4 sheets holly vine pattern (#634824)

Materials:
- Alphabet stickers (#217003)
- Clear domed stickers (#557420)
- Fibers
- Foam-core board
- Gold trim
- Red ribbon
- Silver brads

Page 119
CHRISTMAS CARD AND ORNAMENT
designed by Sue Elred
CARD
Papers:
- 1 sheet hunter green cardstock (#630987)

- 1 sheet swirl pattern (#632653)
- 1 sheet vine paper pattern (#634824)

Materials:
- Christmas stickers (#554290)
- Fibers
- Gold marker

ORNAMENT
Papers:
- 1 sheet red suede pattern (#633681)

Materials:
- Christmas stickers (#554290)
- Red cord
- Red ribbon
- White tassel

Pages 120–121
BUTTON PLACE SETTINGS
designed by Judi Vaughan
HEART *(on page 120)*
Papers:
- 2 sheets button pattern (#636417)

Materials:
- Cream buttons
- Cream ribbon
- Greenery

SCONCE *(on page 121)*
Papers:
- 1 sheet script and button pattern (#636538)

Materials:
- Cream buttons
- Cream ribbon
- Flowers
- Greenery

Thank You

I have been blessed over the years to have experienced great success while doing what I love. K&Company truly is a labor of love. None of this would be possible without hundreds of people who help K&Company thrive every day, and I sincerely thank all of them for their hard work and dedication. In addition, several people helped me create the wonderful ideas found in this, our very first book, and I want to acknowledge them.

Special thanks go to Pamela Lange, a long-time, dedicated colleague at K&Company whose creativity and enthusiasm for this book helped keep me going, and to Jo Packham, owner of Chapelle Ltd., who made it all possible. And of course, all of us at K&Company send heartfelt thanks to the scrapbookers, along with a pledge to continue providing you with products designed to inspire and motivate as you preserve memories of generations past and present, for all generations to come.

ACKNOWLEDGEMENTS

Fiskars Brands, Inc.

AccuCut

Henkel Consumer Adhesives, Inc.

Rollabind, L.L.C.

Jewell Craft

Magic Mesh

About the Artists

Elizabeth Brownd

For years, Elizabeth Brownd has collected antique prints, old letters and newspapers, books and vintage fabrics. As she works composing a collage, handpainted details are layered in with pressed flowers and leaves. Elizabeth studied design at the University of Connecticut and pursued further graduate work in art at Otis Parsons School of Design. Her designs appear on calenders, wallpaper, books, and decorative accessories.

Tim Coffey

From his home near the farms and rolling countryside of Atkinson, New Hampshire, Tim Coffey brings his homespun and wonderfully textured artwork into lines designed exclusively for K&Company. In addition to K&Company, his artwork has been reproduced in many forms including children's books, baby bedding, fabric, greeting cards, and writing journals. His artwork invites people of all ages to enjoy the simple pleasures of life.

Pamela Lange

Pamela has worked for K&Company since its beginning seven years ago. Pamela has brought enthusiasm and experience in crafting that has served K&Company well. She enjoys working with customers and has experience in many craft medias. She designs scrapbook layouts for our shows, classes and idea booklets. She also creates cards and various other products using our papers and stickers. Pamela works along with our product development team and is always the first one to try out our new lines.

Tracey Niehues

Kansas City designer Tracey Niehues grew up in a small town, and the memories of that tight-knit community influence her life, and her Life's Journey layouts. Like Kay Stanley, Tracey was introduced to scrapbooking by her mother. With Life's Journey, her first design work for K&Company, Tracey has created pages filled with meaning, and with love. A popular design teacher, Tracey encourages you to enjoy the creative process, and the many beautiful papers and embellishments in this classic line.

Brenda Walton

From her Northern California studio overlooking a bountiful garden, Brenda Walton creates a diverse range of licensed products from scrapbooking collections and rubber stamps to stationery, dessertware and accessories for the home and garden. Over the years, she has designed scrapbooking collections, photo albums, rubber stamp sets, and wallpaper borders inspired by her love of gardening, her appreciation of the value of enduring friendships, and her fondness for American folk art and European country themes.

Index